HELLE BENEDIKTE NEIGAARD

easy knit dishcloths

LEARN TO KNIT STITCH
BY STITCH
WITH MODERN
STASHBUSTER
PROJECTS

Creative Publishing
international

Brimming with creative inspiration, how-to projects, and useful information to enrich your everyday life, Quarto Knows is a favorite destination for those pursuing their interests and passions. Visit our site and dig deeper with our books into your area of interest: Quarto Creates, Quarto Cooks, Quarto Homes, Quarto Lives, Quarto Drives, Quarto Explores, Quarto Gifts, or Quarto Kids.

First published in the United States of America in 2017 by Creative Publishing international, an imprint of The Quarto Group, 401 Second Avenue North, Suite 310, Minneapolis, MN 55401, USA.
T (612) 344-8100 F (612) 344-8692 QuartoKnows.com

Creative Publishing international titles are also available at discount for retail, wholesale, promotional, and bulk purchase. For details, contact the Special Sales Manager by email at specialsales@quarto.com or by mail at The Quarto Group, Attn: Special Sales Manager, 401 Second Avenue North, Suite 310, Minneapolis, MN 55401, USA.

10 9 8 7 6 5 4 3 2

ISBN: 978-1-58923-956-2

Library of Congress Cataloging-in-Publication Data available.

Translation by Sinéad Quirke Køngerskov
Page layout and design: Anja Søe Jensen
Cover image and photography: David Bering/Montgomery

Printed in China

why knit a dishcloth?

First of all, knitting is, as the Danes say, *hyggeligt*. Knitting is cozy and relaxing—you can unwind from your busy, everyday life and enjoy the meditative effect of the rhythmically moving yarn and needles, while you also get the satisfaction of creating something yourself.

And you even get to help take care of the environment, because your knitted cloths don't contain any micro plastic!

One of the benefits of knitting your own cloths is that you get to choose the colors—and, fortunately, there is a huge range of colors available in cotton yarn. So depending on whether your cloth is to match your tea towel, dishwashing brush, coffee machine, or something else entirely, you're guaranteed to find the right color.

Cloths are also a good way to use up excess yarn, because almost all cloths look good with stripes. Put your favorite colors together. About 145 yards (132 m) of yarn is used per cloth in this book—so you'll automatically have yarn left over each time you knit a cloth.

You can, of course, use the cloths yourself, but they also make nice hostess or token gifts—who wouldn't like to receive a nice home-knitted cloth?

In this book, you'll find thirteen different patterns for cloths, so there is something for everyone, from the beginner to the experienced knitter: cloths knit in simple garter stitch to cloths knit with geometric patterns and crossing stitches. Some of the patterns include diagrams, and all the techniques you need are explained in the first part of the book.

If you share your creations on Instagram, please tag the picture with #quartoknows #quartocreates #dishcloths #knitting #cozy #hygge.

Happy knitting!

contents

materials

. . . .

YARN:

All the paterns use fingering weigh yarn (cyc 1, superfine) in 100 percent cotton.

Two yarns were used to make the sample shown. Mayflower Cotton 8-186 yards (170 m) per 50 g, Sandnes Mandarin Petit-197 yards (180 m) per 50 g. Both yarns are available in a wide range of colors.

NEEDLES:

The cloths are knit on size 2 (3 mm) needles or on a needle necessary to obtain the desired gauge.

GAUGE:

26-27 sts per 4" (10 cm) in stockinette stitch.

SIZE:

The cloths in the book are knit so as to be square, measuring about 10" (25 cm) on each side.

If you don't want a square cloth, just keep knitting until the cloth is the right length for you.

kitchen handtowels

It's easy to convert the patterns if you would like to knit a kitchen hand-towel to match your new cloth.

You can, of course, knit the towel to exactly the size you want, but, in each pattern, I've written how many stitches you need to cast on if you would like a kitchen towel measuring about 14" (35 cm) in width. I would suggest a length of about 18" (45 cm), but it's entirely up to you.

When you bind off the last stitch, cut the yarn, but allow for a tail of about 12" (30 cm) to hang from the handtowel. Then you can crochet a chain of single crochet stitches and attach it to the towel, so you have a nice loop for hanging up your towel.

patterns and edges

At the beginning of each pattern, you can see how many stitches you need for a cloth measuring approximately 10" (25 cm) in width. For those who want a larger cloth, I've also included the stitch ratio for additional stitches, so it's easy for you to calculate a larger cloth.

Many of the cloths are edged in garter stitch—in other words, the cloth is started by knitting a number of rows in knit stitch, so the cloth has garter stitch on both sides. I prefer narrow edges, but if you want a wider edge, simply knit some more rows at the beginning and end of the cloth and include more edging stitches at both sides of the cloth.

Edging stitches are included in both the written instructions and the diagrams.

gauge

Gauge is a measure of the number of stitches you knit per 4" (10 cm). Quite simply it means you knit a sample of 4" by 4" (10 by 10 cm), and then measure it with a tape measure to see how many stitches you used for that 4" (10 cm). Most of the patterns include the gauge from which the pattern was worked out.

Gauge can end up being different from person to person, even if you use the same yarn and the same needles. Therefore, it can be a good idea to knit a swatch and check your gauge, especially if you knit clothing where the exact size of your finished work is important. But when knitting cloths, it's perhaps less important to hit 10" by 10" (25 x 25 cm) exactly, so you can skip knitting the swatch, if you like.

If your gauge shows that you have too many stitches per 4" (10 cm), it could be a good idea to go up a needle size. This typically happens if your knitting is a little tight.

If, on the other hand, you have too few stitches per 4 " (10 cm), it's probably because you're knitting a little too loosely, and so you may want to go down a needle size.

If you are a beginner, you can find explanations of the basic techniques used in the patterns on the pages that follow.

There is also plenty of help available online. For example, there are many knitting videos to be found on YouTube, where you can easily see how to knit the different stitches.

The patterns here have been awarded 1, 2, or 3 stars, according to their level of difficulty.

✴   You are most comfortable with knit and purl stitches used in a simple and practical way.

✴✴   You feel comfortable with knit and purl stitches and would like to use them in combinations that are a little more challenging.

✴✴✴ You want to move beyond knit and purl and throw yourself into more advanced techniques, such as cable stitches and slip stitches.

casting on

 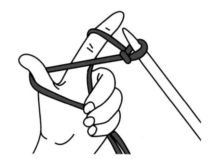 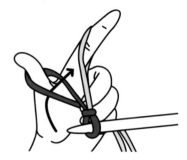

1. Make a loop on the right needle and allow a tail of yarn to hang. Generally the yarn should be about three times as long as the dishcloth is wide, i.e., about 30" (75 cm).

2. Place your left thumb and index finger between the yarn ends. Wind the end of the yarn around your index finger, and the rest of the yarn end around your thumb.

3. Use your other fingers to pull the yarn tight. Turn your palm upward, and form a *V* with the yarn. *Work the knitting needle up through the thumb loop.

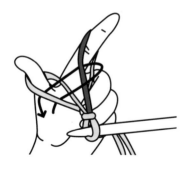 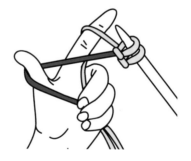 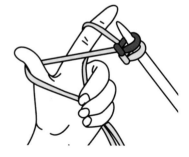

3. Work the needle over the first part of the loop on your index finger and pull the yarn through the thumb loop.

5. Release the thumb loop, and place your thumb in the V-position again with the yarn wound around your thumb.

6. Now tighten the stitch you made on the needle. Repeat from * until you have the desired number of stitches.

knit stitch • k

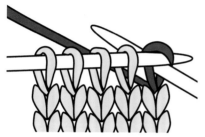

1. Insert the right needle into the first stitch on the left needle. Work the needle in from the front (from left to right) into the front part of the stitch.

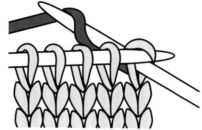

2. Now pick up the yarn from your left index finger with the right needle.

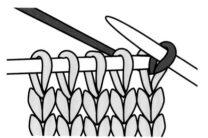

3. Pull the new loop through the stitch with the tip of the right needle.

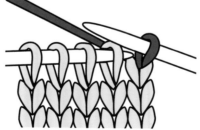

4. Let the stitch slip off the left needle. You now have a new stitch on the right needle.

ABBREVIATIONS

st(s)	= stitch(es)
k	= knit
p	= purl
co	= cast on
k2tog	= knit two together
ssk	= slip, slip, knit
rs	= right side
ws	= wrong side
ca	= circa (about or approximately)
yo	= yard over

There is also a little rhyme to help you remember the knit stitch:

In through the front door,
Once round the back,
Out through the window,
And off jumps Jack.

purl stitch • p

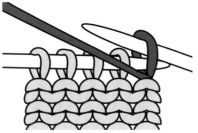

1. Insert the right needle into the first stitch on the left needle. Work the needle in from behind (from right to left) into the front part of the stitch.

2. Work the right needle behind the yarn and turn it to the right in front of the yarn. You have now formed a loop on the needle.

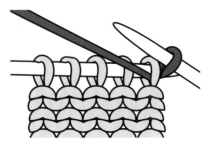

3. Pull the loop through the stitch with the tip of the right needle.

4. Let the stitch slip off the left needle. You now have a new stitch on the right needle.

yarn over • yo

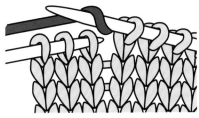

1. Wrap the yarn over the right nee dle by placing the yarn in front of the cloth, as if you were going to knit purl, and knit the next stitch.

slip stitch • sl st

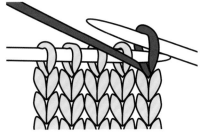
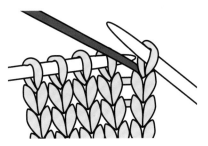

1. Insert the right needle into the first stitch on the left needle. Work the needle in from behind (from right to left) into the front part of the stitch, as if you were going to knit purl.

2. Let the stitch slip over onto the right needle without knitting it.

knit two together • k2tog

 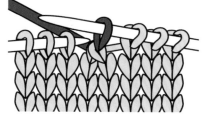

1. Insert the right needle through the first two stitches on the left needle, just as when your go to knit a stitch.

2. Pull the yarn through and let the two stitches slip off the needle.

slip, slip, knit • ssk

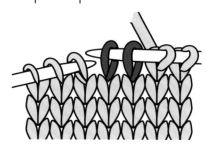 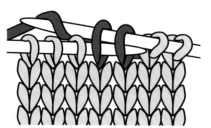

1. Slip off two stitches—one at a time —from the left needle onto the right.

2. Work the left needle in through the front part of the two stitches. The stitches are now turned around, knit them together into one stitch.

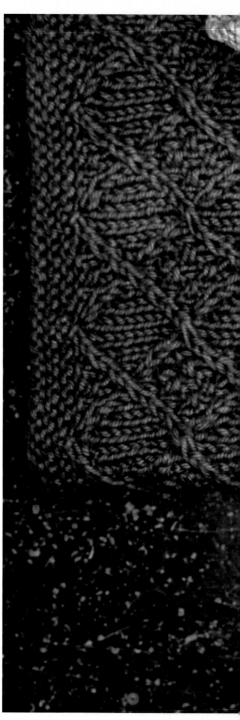

patterns

the simple cloth *

If you are a beginner or you just want to knit something that's simple, then knit a cloth in garter stitch—a simple and functional cloth in your favorite color!

YARN	Fingering weight yarn (cyc 1, Super Fine), 100 percent cotton; samples knit with Sandnes Mandarin Petit and Mayflower Cotton 8
YARDAGE	ca. 130 yards (118 m)
NEEDLES	size 2 (3 mm)
SIZE	10" x 10" (25 x 25 cm)

If you would like a larger cloth, just cast on a number of extra stitches.

HANDTOWEL	100 sts to start
YARDAGE	ca. 394 yards (360 m)
SIZE	14" x 18" (35 x 45 cm)

1. Cast 75 sts onto a size 2 needle, and knit all rows.

2. Continue until the cloth measures 10" (25 cm), or the desired length, and bind off. Weave in the yarn ends.

broken rib *

This cloth, knit in broken rib, is easy to knit once you get started. It is a classic pattern.

YARN   Fingering weight yarn (cyc 1, Super Fine), 100 percent cotton; samples knit with Sandnes Mandarin Petit white [1002] and cinnamon brown [2336]

YARDAGE   ca. 130 yards (118 m)

NEEDLES   Size 2 (3 mm)

SIZE   10" x 10" (25 x 25 cm)

HANDTOWEL   101 sts to start

YARDAGE   ca. 394 yards (360 m)

SIZE   14" x 18" (35 x 45 cm)

If you would like a larger cloth, just cast on an extra number of stitches (divisible by 2).

1. Cast 75 sts onto a size 2 needle.

2. Knit pattern:

   Row 1: p1, *k1, p1; repeat from * to end of row.

   Row 2: Knit.

3. Repeat rows 1 and 2 until the work measures 10" (25 cm), or the desired length, and bind off. Weave in the yarn ends.

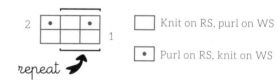

Knit on RS, purl on WS

Purl on RS, knit on WS

broken basketweave **

This fine weave pattern makes a sweet and usable cloth, and once you get going, the pattern is easy to knit.

YARN	Fingering weight yarn (cyc 1, Super Fine), 100 percent cotton; sample knit with Mayflower Cotton 8 in light green [1486]	**HANDTOWEL**	100 sts to start
		YARDAGE	ca. 372 yards (340 m)
		SIZE	14" x 18" (35 x 45 cm)
YARDAGE	ca. 141 yards (129 m)		
NEEDLES	size 2 (3 mm)		
SIZE	10" x 10" (25 x 25 cm)		

If you would like a larger cloth, just cast on an extra number of stitches (divisible by 6).

1. Cast on 76 stitches, and knit 6 rows.

2. Knit pattern:

    Row 1 (RS): k3, *p1, k2; repeat from * to the last 4 sts. p1, k3.

    Rows 2, 4, 6, and 8: K3, purl to the last 3 sts, k3.

    Row 3: k3, *p4, k2; repeat from * to the last 7 sts, p4, k3.

    Row 5: as row 1.

    Row 7: k3, *p1, k2, p3; repeat from * to the last 7 sts, p1, k2, p1, k3.

3. Repeat rows 1–8 until the cloth measures ca. 10" (24 cm), or the desired length.

Knit 6 rows, and bind off. Weave in the yarn ends.

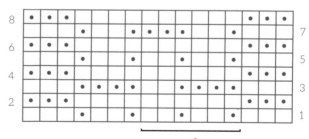

repeat

Knit on RS, purl on WS

Purl on RS, knit on WS

a cloth with ripples **

This homey rippled cloth has a cozy pattern on both sides.

YARN Fingering weight yarn (CYC 1, Super Fine), 100 percent cotton; sample knit with Mayflower Cotton 8 in natural [1401]

YARDAGE ca. 148 yards (136 m)

NEEDLES size 2 (3 mm)

SIZE 10" x 10" (25 x 25 cm)

HANDTOWEL 102 sts to start

YARDAGE ca. 372 yards (340 m)

SIZE 14" x 18" (35 x 45 cm)

If you would like a larger cloth, just cast on an extra number of stitches (divisible by 8).

1. Cast on 78 sts, and knit 3 rows.

2. Knit pattern:

   Rows 1 and 3 (WS): k6, *p2, k6; repeat from * to the last 8 sts, p2, k6.

   Row 2: k2, p4, *k2, p6; repeat from * to that last 8 sts, k2, p4, k2.

   Row 4: knit.

   Rows 5 and 7: k10, *p2, k6; repeat from * to the last 12 sts, p2, k10.

   Row 6: k2, p8, *k2, p6; repeat from * to the last 12 sts, k2, p8, k2.

   Row 8: knit.

3. Repeat rows 1-8 until the cloth measures 10" (25 cm) or the desired length. Knit 3 rows and bind off. Weave in the yarn ends.

cable stitch ***

This cable stitch cloth seems complicated, but it's actually very easy to knit.

YARN	Fingering weight yarn (cyc 1, Super Fine), 100 percent cotton; sample knit with Mayflower Cotton 8 in mint [1492], or Mandarin Petit peach [4015]
YARDAGE	ca. 145 yard (132 m)
NEEDLES	size 2 (3 mm)
SIZE	10" x 10" (25 x 25 cm)

If you would like a larger cloth, just cast on an extra number of stitches (divisible by 5).

HANDTOWEL	105 sts to start
YARDAGE	ca. 383 yards (350 m)
SIZE	14" x 18" (35 x 45 cm)

1. Cast on 75 sts.

2. Knit pattern:

    Row 1: k4, *p2, k3; repeat from *, finish with p2, k4.

    Row 2: k1, p3, *k2, p3; repeat from *, finish with k2, p3, k1.

    Row 3: k1, *sl 1 st, k2, lift the slipped st over the 2 sts just knitted, p2; repeat from *, Finish with sl 1 st, k2, lift the slipped st over the 2 sts just knitted, k1.

    Row 4: k1, *p1, yo, p1, k2; repeat from *, finish with p1, yo, p1, k1.

3. Repeat rows 1-4 until the cloth measures 10" (25 cm), or the desired length, and bind off. Weave in the yarn ends.

zigzag pattern **

This zigzag cloth is fun to knit and results in the same pattern on both sides.

YARN	Fingering weight yarn (cyc 1, Super Fine), 100 percent cotton; samples knit with Sandnes Mandarin Petit in corn yellow [2015] and dark gray [5870]
YARDAGE	ca. 142 yards (129 m)
NEEDLES	size 2 (3 mm)
SIZE	10" x 10" (25 x 25 cm)

HANDTOWEL	97 sts to start
YARDAGE	ca. 394 yards (360 m)
SIZE	14" x 18" (35 x 45 cm)

If you would like a larger cloth, just cast on an extra number of stitches (divisible by 18).

1. Cast on 79 sts, and knit 6 rows.

2. Knit pattern:

    Rows 1 and 3: k3, p1, *[k2, p2] twice, k1, [p2, k2] twice, p1; repeat from * to the last 3 sts, k3.

    Rows 2 and 4: k3, *k1, [p2, k2] twice, p1, [k2, p2] twice; repeat from * to the last 4 sts, k1, k3.

    Rows 5 and 7: k3, p1, *p1, [k2, p2] twice, p1, [k2, p2] twice; repeat from * to the last 3 sts, k3.

    Rows 6 and 8: k3, *[k2, p2] twice, k3, p2, k2, p2, k1; repeat from * to the last 4 sts, k1, k3.

    Rows 9 and 11: k3, k1, *[p2, k2] twice, p1, [k2, p2] twice, k1; repeat from * to the last 3 sts, k3.

    Rows 10 and 12: k3, *p1, [k2, p2] twice, k1, [p2, k2] twice; repeat from * to the last 4 sts, p1, k3.

    Rows 13 and 15: k3, k1, *k1, [p2, k2] twice, k1, [p2, k2] twice; repeat from * to the last 3 sts, k3.

    Rows 14 and 16: k3, *[p2, k2] twice, p3, k2, p2, k2, p1; repeat from * to the last 4 sts, p1, k3.

3. Repeat rows 1–16 until the cloth measures 10" (25 cm), or the desired length. Knit 6 rows, and bind off. Weave in the yarn ends.

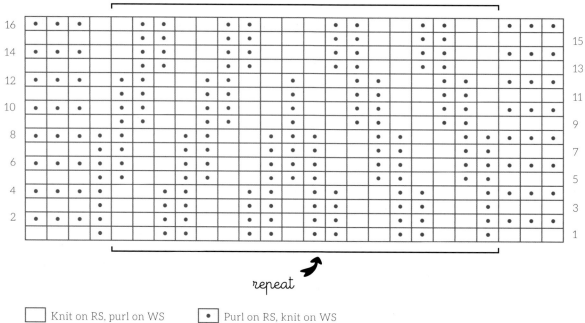

Knit on RS, purl on WS • Purl on RS, knit on WS

espalier pattern ***

This beautiful espalier pattern gives a refined cloth, which would make a nice hostess gift.

YARN	Fingering weight yarn (cyc 1, Super Fine), 100 percent cotton; samples knit with Mayflower Cotton 8 in jean blue [1421], or light gray [1440]
YARDAGE	ca. 148 yards (136 m)
NEEDLES	size 2 (3 mm)
SIZE	10" x 10" (25 x 25 cm)

If you would like a larger cloth, just cast on an extra number of stitches (divisible by 8).

HANDTOWEL	101 sts to start
YARDAGE	ca. 372 yards (340 m)
SIZE	14" x 18" (35 x 45 cm)

SPECIAL ABBREVIATIONS

C2R: (cross to the right)—knit 1 st on the front of the 2nd st on the left needle, knit 1 st on the back of the 1st st on the left needle, and let both sts slip off the left needle.

C2L: (cross to the left)—knit 1 st on the back on the 2nd st on the right needle, knit 1 on the front of the 1st st on the left needle, and let both sts slip off the left needle.

C3R: (right cross over 3 sts)—now knit the 3rd, 2nd, and 1st sts on the left needle, and then let all 3 sts slip off the needle at the same time.

1. Cast 77 sts onto a size 2 needle and knit 6 rows.

2. Knit pattern:

   Row 1: k3, k1, p1, *[k1, p1] twice, C3R, p1; repeat from * to the last 8 sts, [k1, p1] twice, k1, k3.

   Rows 2, 4, 6, 8, 10, 12: k3, knit as shown (k over k, p over p) to the last 3 sts, k3.

   Row 3: k3, C2L, *k1, p1, k1, C2R, k1, C2L; repeat from * to the last 8 sts, k1, p1, k1, C2R, k3.

   Row 5: k3, k1, *C2L, p1, C2R, k3; repeat from * to the last 9 sts, C2L, p1, C2R, k1, k3.

   Row 7: k3, k2, *C3R, k5; repeat from * to the last 8 sts, C3R, k2, k3.

   Row 9: k3, k1, *C2R, p1, C2L, p3; repeat from * to the last 9 sts, C2R, p1, C2L, k1, k3.

   Row 11: k3, C2R, *p1, k1, p1, x2L, k1, C2R; repeat from * to the last 8 sts, p1, k1, p1, C2L, k3.

3. Repeat rows 1–12 until the cloth measures ca. 10" (25 cm), and finish with either pattern row 1 or 7 (a right side row), knit 5 rows, and bind off. Weave in the yarn ends.

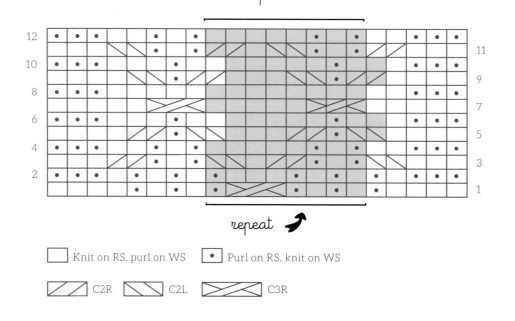

repeat ➤

| | Knit on RS, purl on WS | • | Purl on RS, knit on WS |

C2R   C2L   C3R

gentle waves ***

These gentle waves change color at each pattern repeat. You can, for example, vary the cloth by switching to a new color each time so you end up with a nice rainbow cloth. The gentle waves also suit a unicolor cloth.

YARN	Fingering weight yarn (cyc 1, Super Fine), 100 percent cotton; samples knit with
YARDAGE	Sandnes Mandarin Petit in jean blue [6543],
NEEDLES	light petrol [6822], and natural [1012]
SIZE	ca. 153 yards (140 m)
	size 2 (3 mm)
	10" x 10" (25 x 25 cm)

HANDTOWEL	103 sts to start
YARDAGE	ca. 394 yards (360 m)
SIZE	14" x 18" (35 x 45 cm)

If you would like a larger cloth, just cast on an extra number of stitches (divisible by 9).

Note:
This pattern uses ssk (slip, slip, knit). See the explanation on pages 15 and 20.

1. Cast 76 sts onto a size 2 needle.

2. Knit pattern:

   Rows 1, 2, and 3: knit.

   Row 4: k2, purl to the last 2 sts, k2.

   Row 5: k2, *k3, [yo, k1] three times, yo, k3; repeat from * to the last 2 sts, k2.

   Row 6: same as row 4.

   Row 7: k2, *[k2tog] twice, k5, [ssk] twice; repeat from * to the last 2 sts, k2.

   Row 8: knit.

3. Repeat rows 1–8, and change color each time you start row 1. Knit until the cloth measures ca. 10" (24 cm), or the desired length—after the last pattern repeat knit 2 rows, and bind off. Weave in the yarn ends.

dragonscale ✳✳✳

This lovely pattern is reminiscent of dragonscales—it looks complicated, but it is very easy to knit.

YARN	Fingering weight yarn (cyc 1, Super Fine), 100 percent cotton; samples knit with
YARDAGE	Sandnes Mandarin Petit in burnt orange
NEEDLES	[2709] and terracotta [4234]
SIZE	ca. 153 yards (140 m)
	size 2 (3 mm)
	10" x 10" (25 x 25 cm)

HANDTOWEL	104 sts to start
YARDAGE	ca. 394 yards (360 m)
SIZE	14" x 18" (35 x 45 cm)

If you would like a larger cloth, just cast on an extra number of stitches (divisible by 4).

1. Cast 76 sts onto a size 2 needle, and knit 5 rows.

2. Knit pattern:

   Rows 1 and 3 (WS): k3, purl to the last 3 sts, k3.

   Row 2: k4, *work the right needle in under the yarn between the newly knitted st and the next st, so an extra loop is formed on the needle; knit the next 2 sts and lift the extra loop over the 2 knitted sts, k2; repeat from * to the last 4 sts, k4.

   Row 4: k6, repeat from * on row 2, and finish the last repetition with k4.

3. Repeat rows 1–4 until cloth measures 10" (25 cm), finish with pattern row 2 or 4 (a RS row), knit 5 rows, and bind off. Weave in the yarn ends.

parallelogram **

This is a nice geometric pattern on both sides of the cloth. You could also vary the pattern by changing the color after each pattern repeat.

YARN	Fingering weight yarn (cyc 1, Super Fine), 100 percent cotton; sample knit with Mayflower Cotton 8 coral [1460]
YARDAGE	ca. 137 yards (125 m)
NEEDLES	size 2 (3 mm)
SIZE	10" x 10" (25 x 25 cm)

HANDTOWEL	104 sts to start
YARDAGE	ca. 372 yards (340 m)
SIZE	14" x 18" (35 x 45 cm)

If you would like a larger cloth, just cast on an extra number of stitches (divisible by 10).

1. Cast 74 sts onto a size 2 needle, and knit 4 rows.

2. Knit pattern:

   Row 1 (RS): k2, *p5, k5; repeat from * to the last 2 sts, k2.

   Row 2: k3, *p5, k5; repeat from * to the last 11 sts, p5, k6.

   Row 3: k2, p3, *k5, p5; repeat from * to the last 9 sts, k5, p2, k2.

   Row 4: k5, *p5, k5; repeat from * to the last 9 sts, p5, k4.

   Row 5: k2, p1, *k5, p5; repeat from * to the last 11 sts, k5, p4, k2.

   Row 6: k2, p4, *k5, p5; repeat from * to the last 8 sts, k5, p1, k2.

   Row 7: k4, *p5, k5; repeat from * to the last 10 sts, p5, k5.

   Row 8: k2, p2, *k5, p5; repeat from * to the last 10 sts, k5, p3, k2.

   Row 9: k6, *p5, k5; repeat from * to the last 8 sts, p5, k3.

   Row 10: k2, *k5, p5; repeat from * to the last 2 sts, k2.

3. Repeat rows 1–10 until the cloth measures ca. 10" (25 cm), or the desired length. Knit 4 rows, and bind off. Weave in the yarn ends.

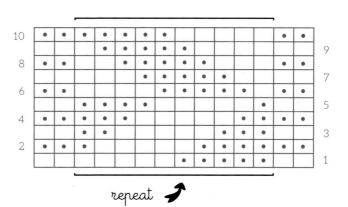

repeat

☐ Knit on RS, purl on WS

• Purl on RS, knit on WS

Note: Chart row 1 establishes the pattern.

reflections **

This cloth has an exciting reflected geometric pattern on both sides.

YARN   Fingering weight yarn (cyc 1, Super Fine), 100 percent cotton; samples knit with Mayflower Cotton 8 in light heather [4622]

YARDAGE   ca. 126 yards (115 m)

NEEDLES   size 2 (3 mm)

SIZE   10" x 10" (25 x 25 cm)

HANDTOWEL   104 sts to start

YARDAGE   ca. 372 yards (340 m)

SIZE   14" x 18" (35 x 45 cm)

If you would like a larger cloth, just cast on an extra number of stitches (divisible by 8).

1. Cast on 76 sts, and knit 4 rows.

2. Knit pattern:

   Row 1: knit.

   Row 2: k2, *k4, p4; repeat from * to the last 2 sts, k2.

   Row 3: k2, p1, *k4, p4; repeat from * to the last 9 sts, k4, p3, k2.

   Row 4: k4, *p4, k4; repeat from * to the last 8 sts, p4, k4.

   Row 5: k2, p3; *k4, p4; repeat from * to the last 7 sts, k4, p1, k2.

   Row 6: k2, *p4, k4; repeat from * to the last 2 sts, k2.

   Row 7: knit.

   Rows 8, 9, 10, and 11: k2, *k4, p4; repeat from * to the last 2 sts, k2.

   Row 12: k2, purl to the last 2 sts, k2.

   Row 13: as row 6.

   Row 14: k3, *p4, k4; repeat from * to the last 9 sts, p4, k5.

   Row 15: k2, p2, *k4, p4; repeat from * to the last 8 sts, k4, p2, k2.

   Row 16: k5, *p4, k4; repeat from * to the last 7 sts, p4, k3.

   Row 17: as row 2.

   Row 18: k2, purl to the last 2 sts, k2.

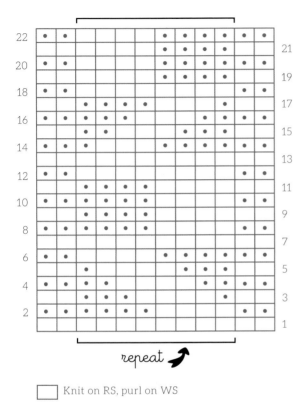

repeat ↗

□ Knit on RS, purl on WS

• Purl on RS, knit on WS

Note: Chart row 1 establishes the pattern.

Rows 19, 20, 21, and 22: k2, *p4, k4; repeat from * to the last 2 sts, k2.

3. Repeat rows 1–22 until the cloth measures ca. 10" 25 cm), or the desired length. Knit 4 rows, and bind off. Weave in the yarn ends.

waffle rib ***

This waffled cloth is perfect for the kitchen, and it is fun to knit.

YARN Fingering weight yarn (cyc 1, Super Fine), 100 percent cotton; samples knit with Sandnes Mandarin Petit in peach [4015] and dark gray [5870]

YARDAGE ca. 153 yards (140 m)

NEEDLES size 2 (3 mm)

SIZE 10" x 10" (25 x 25 cm)

HANDTOWEL 103 sts to start

YARDAGE ca. 395 yards (360 m)

SIZE 14" x 18" (35 x 45 cm)

If you would like a larger cloth, just cast on an extra number of stitches (divisible by 4).

1. Cast 75 sts onto a size 2 needle, and knit 4 rows.

2. Knit pattern:

    Row 1 (RS): k3, *1 sl st, k3; repeat from * to the end of the row.

    Rows 2, 4, 6, and 8: k3, *p1, k3; repeat from * to the end of the row.

    Rows 3, 5, and 7: k3; *1 sl st, p3; repeat from * to the last 4 sts, 1 sl st, k3.

    Row 9: as row 1.

    Row 10: k3, purl to the last 3 sts, k3.

3. Repeat rows 1–10 until the cloth measures 10" (25 cm), or the desired length—finish with row 8. Knit 4 rows, and bind off. Weave in the yarn ends.

blue stripes *

This cloth has classic blue sari-stripes at each end. You can combine colors as you wish, and add extra stripes, if you like.

YARN	Fingering weight yarn (cyc 1, Super Fine), 100 percent cotton; samples knit with Sandnes Mandarin Petit in white [1002] and jean blue [6543]
YARDAGE	ca. 134 yards (122 m)
NEEDLES	size 2 (3 mm)
SIZE	10" x 10" (25 x 25 cm)

If you would like a larger cloth, just cast on extra stitches.

HANDTOWEL	100 sts to start
YARDAGE	ca. 394 yards (360 m)
SIZE	14" x 18" (35 x 45 cm)

1. Cast on 74 sts in white yarn.

2. Knit 4 rows, and then knit stockinette stitch with 3 edge stitches on each side:

   Row 1: knit.

   Row 2: k3, purl to the last 3 sts, k3.

3. Knit the striped pattern as follows:

   2 white rows
   2 blue rows
   2 white rows
   4 blue rows
   2 white rows
   2 blue rows

4. Now continue in white until the cloth measures 2" (5 cm) smaller than the desired length.

   2 blue rows
   2 white rows
   4 blue rows
   2 white rows
   2 blue rows
   2 white rows

5. Now knit 4 rows, and bind off. Weave in the yarn ends.